25th

Anniversary

Circle of Miracles

AN INTERSPIRITUAL COMMUNITY

Rev. Mike Wanner

Table of Contents

Introduction

The Circle of Miracles has long been a treasure for me. I met the founder shortly after taking a Reiki I Class in 1993.

I attended the Reiki Share of the founder of Circle - Hannelore Z. Goodwin, at a Holistic Center in Langhorne. I continued to study with her as she continued her studies.

In August of 1995, she was preparing a graduation project for a Life Enrichment program she was taking at the time. The plan was to conduct a Spiritual Ministry Event that became what we now know as a Celebration.

The event, attended by family and friends, was Joyous!
One of those friends encouraged her to make it an ongoing Ministry. She resisted, but over time, she revisited the suggestion. The Ministry grew in her home, and the rest is history.

I want to share the Circle of Miracles' message with the world, and I cannot do that alone. I am asking for help through this book, and I invite you to share all you know about and wish to create in Circle and invite all you know.

Blessings
Rev. Mike Wanner

Be Welcome Here

Circle of Miracles Offers:

- Sunday Celebration

- Reiki Share and Training

- Ordination through our Interfaith Ministry School

- Courses and Workshops

- Community Outreach Opportunities

- Weddings, Memorials, & Other Ceremonies

- And so much more!

1 - Circle of Miracles

WHO ARE WE?

Circle of Miracles is a welcoming, inclusive spiritual community, grounded in Love, Harmony and Peace. We lovingly provide a safe place for connection with the Divine, as it flows within the individual and is shared and held as sacred by the community. Recognizing that there are many paths to All That Is, we practice acceptance and generosity as we share and learn from each other's journeys.

OUR MISSION

A loving community where we nurture and express the unfolding of spirituality in service to the world.

OUR VISION

To ignite sparks of vibrant energy that unite the world in peace, love and joy.

OUR VALUES

Circle of Miracles:

- Honors each individual's unique path to the Divine.

- Explores and practices spirituality through study, prayer and meditation.

- Acknowledges that we manifest through thoughts, words, and actions; therefore, we are mindful of what we create.

- Creates Love, Harmony, Peace and Abundance for all through Divine Guidance.

- Honors everyone with Respect, Generosity and Loving Kindness.

- Recognizes that no one needs fixing, allowing everyone to affect their own destiny.

- Serves humanity and our planet by encouraging the use of individual gifts and talents for the highest good for all.

- Acknowledges and respects Mother Earth and the magnificence of all Creation.

- Celebrates that we are all One.

2 - Our Roots

How Circle of Miracles Began

Reverend Hannelore Goodwin, the founder of Circle of Miracles, was born in Germany during World War II. She narrowly and miraculously escaped death several times during bombing raids. At 12 years old, during her First Holy Communion, she had an emotional, spiritual experience in church and vowed to dedicate her life to God. At the age of eighteen, she emigrated to the United States, got married, had children, and her promise lay dormant. Ultimately, she fulfilled part of her promise by becoming an ordained metaphysical minister, although she was not sure how she was going to use this experience.

In 1984, Hannelore divorced, and in 1987, she married Bob Goodwin. Through a series of miracles, they were able to purchase 13+ acres of wooded property in Wycombe, PA, where they built a beautiful Alpine Chalet style home with a large downstairs great room surrounded on three sides by windows facing into the woods.

By this time, Hannelore had become a Reiki Master Teacher, and this new space provided fabulous surroundings for teaching Reiki and other workshops and classes. Hannelore's public life had begun. She referred to this as "coming out of the cocoon" as her true "butterfly" Self emerged. *Healing Alternatives*, the forerunner to Circle of Miracles, was born.

In 1995, she began taking a series of classes at Landmark Education, which culminated in a course called the Self Expression and Leadership Program (SELP). To pass, each student had to develop and execute a project serving mankind. The project had to be self-sustaining, which meant that after it was put into life, it could continue on its own, being run by another person or persons. Some of her SELP classmates suggested she plan a nondenominational celebration, one that reflected her belief that many doors led to spirit, and one door was just as valid as the next. The idea blossomed. The first Celebration of spirit took place on Saturday, July 22, 1995. After it concluded, Hannelore thought she was done, but spirit had other ideas!

It took a great deal of convincing from spiritual friends, but finally, the date for the first continuous Sunday Celebration was set: Thanksgiving weekend, Sunday, November 26, 1995. An intricate part of Hannelore's spiritual philosophy was deeply rooted in *A Course in Miracles,* and so the Celebration was named Circle of Miracles.

A few years later, Hannelore answered another inner directive calling her to create a Circle of Miracles Ministry School. Her vision was to train ministers as a way to expand Circle without the necessity of acquiring huge buildings. The nondenominational philosophy of the Celebration could be brought into any living room, rehab center, retirement home, even prisons.

Finding A New Home

As time went on, Sunday Services became very popular, making it increasingly difficult to accommodate parking on the Wycombe property. Ultimately, in 2007, the township gave notification that gatherings could not continue without a permit. Unfortunately, there were too many hurdles, and so it became obvious that a new home was needed for Circle of Miracles.

Circle of Miracles currently resides in a beautiful colonial style building built in 1857. Located at 10 Beulah Rd. in New Britain, PA, it is the former sight of the Pearl S. Buck Adoption Center. We at Circle of Miracles feel blessed to be holding our sacred services in the space where many children found their way to loving homes. In fact, a few people have come to services and commented that this place was where they came to adopt their child.

In addition, one of the graduates of Circle's Ministry School rented this space when she opened her spiritual practice with another graduate and her husband, a horticulturist. The organization was named "Seeds for Change" and hosted classes both in spirituality and horticulture. This became the synchronistic connection that resulted in Circle finding this wonderful space to call home.

Rev. Bob Goodwin – The Rock

Rev. Bob Goodwin (Hannelore's husband) was always very supportive of Hannelore and Circle. He generously agreed to allow the bottom part of his home to become a sacred haven for people to explore their individual connection to spirit and interpretation of God.

He personally joined the Ministry School and graduated with the class of 2007. Bob's smiling face was always the first to greet people as they arrived for Sunday Celebration. His warm, welcoming hugs were an anticipated gift every week. Bob initiated the "Spiritual Seed" segment at the beginning of each

Celebration by reading short, meaningful and often amusing quotations about community, spirituality and love. He continued practice until July 2014, just weeks before he transitioned. His most favorite story was:

Keep Your Fork – the Best is Yet to Come!

There was a woman who had been diagnosed with a terminal illness and had been given three months to live. As she was getting her things in order, she contacted her pastor and had him come to her house to discuss certain aspects of her final wishes. She told him which songs she wanted sung during the service, what scriptures she would like read, and what outfit she wanted to be buried in. The woman also requested to be buried with her favorite Bible. Not to mention, she wanted to be buried with a fork too.

Everything was in order and the pastor was preparing to leave when the woman suddenly remembered something very important to her. "There's one more thing," she said excitedly. "What's that?" came the pastor's reply. "This is very important," the woman continued… "I want to be buried with a fork in my right hand." The pastor stood looking at the woman, not knowing quite what to say. "That surprises you, doesn't it?" the woman asked. "Well, to be honest, I'm puzzled by the request," said the pastor. The woman explained. "In all my years of attending church socials and potluck dinners, I always remember that when the dishes of the main course were being cleared, someone would inevitably lean over and say, "keep your fork." It was my favorite part because I knew that something better was coming... like velvety chocolate cake or deep-dish apple pie. Something wonderful, and with substance!

So, I just want people to see me there in that casket with a fork in my hand and I want them to wonder 'What's with the fork?' Then, I want you to tell them: "Keep Your Fork"... "The best is yet to come." The pastor's eyes welled up with tears of joy as he hugged the woman goodbye. He knew this would be one of the last times he would see her before her death: but he also knew that the woman had a better grasp of heaven that he did. She KNEW that something better was coming.

In 2015, Hannelore transitioned as well, but Circle of Miracles lives on, as do the Circles created by graduates. Hannelore's dream, and her promise to God have been fulfilled.

We are deeply grateful to Reverends Hannelore and Bob Goodwin for their vision and years of dedication, giving Circle of Miracles a solid foundation upon which to grow.

3 - Ministry School

Circle of Miracles School of Ministries

Approximately four years after the start of Circle of Miracles Sunday Celebration, Reverend Hannelore's Goodwin had a new vision.

As she connected with more and more students in her Reiki classes, she observed a growing interest in universal spirituality and a desire for connection with like-minded souls. Rather than invest in a building to expand local outreach, Hannelore envisioned the future of Circle of Miracles to be "Church Without Walls". She, along with a diverse set of spiritual teachers from the community, developed a curriculum that would prepare others to become ordained ministers in order to spread their gifts of universal light and love into the world.

Circle of Miracles Ministries, Inc. was founded in 1999 and the Articles of Incorporation state we are:

A Church, dedicated but not limited to:

- …the research and teaching of metaphysics, spiritual science, and philosophy in correlation with the natural revelations of science and demonstrations of religion as they pertain to the aspirations of man, spiritual and mystical,

- …seeking and finding the spiritual truth within oneself, where God can be found,

- …spiritual counseling, and worship services, to present the Spiritual Truths and Realities,

- …fostering spiritual and religious worship celebrating the divine presence in ALL,

- ...offering courses of study in the principles of the spiritual and metaphysical ministry and of the Founder,

- ...educating and ordaining ministers based upon the beliefs of the Founder.

The saying "if you make it they will come" is definitely true. The first class curiously consisted of 12 students, each coming for a different reason. Some came for the self-inquiry or to learn more about other Religions, while others wanted to start their own Sunday celebration or healing center. To date, 151 Ministers have been Ordained and 4 more will graduate in January 2021.

Once graduated, Circle ministers share their individual gifts and training in many different ways. Some have healing practices, some wedding ministries; some have taken their ministries into prisons, retirement communities, nursing homes, and into churches. They all graduate with a deeper connection to the Source within their life and pledge to "walk the walk and talk the talk" in their daily lives with family, friends and colleagues.

The program has evolved several times over the years, yet always remains true to its founding principles. The types of experiential workshops and variety of available resources are continuously updated, and new instructors keep the school vibrantly alive and relevant to what is happening in the world.

Today, Circle of Miracles Ministry School assists students with the development of a deeper connection to the Self and thus, to the Source of All That Is. The curriculum encompasses an understanding of diverse religious, cultural practices and spiritual paths, all leading toward the realization that we are not a separate self, but a unique expression of the Singular Reality one may choose to call God, All That Is, Source or whatever label is most meaningful to them.

Our graduated ministers are legally ordained and empowered to create and perform original and unique sacred ceremonies: weddings, funerals, baby welcoming/naming, ritual celebrations, and more.

Classes begin about every two years in the fall. The course runs about 15 months. If you are interested in more information, please consider setting up an appointment to talk with a member of the faculty.

To request a catalog or application, please email info@circleofmiracles.org or call 267-218-4254.

Celebrating Our Next Graduates

We Have Four students Graduating January, 2021

Melodie Gordon

I have a deep love and connection to the land and to people who struggle to find their path. Through my experiences in ministry school I have had the opportunity to rediscover and polish my true passions. I am drawn to assisting the younger generation in finding their way.

After I graduate, I plan to continue my education with CPE training. My ultimate goal is to become a Chaplain for incarcerated youth. Currently that position does not exist for clergy of any kind.

I also have a passion for supporting those who have been abused. I donate my time as a chaplain to a nonprofit that provides shelter for those affected by human trafficking. Presently, I am pursuing a volunteer position at A Woman's Place as an interfaith chaplain, again, a position that does not currently exist.

With the skills I have gained through ministry school, I feel empowered to seek and express the passions of my soul. By doing so I hope to expand the perception of what a minister can be in settings traditionally reserved for a singular set of beliefs.

Melodie Gordon

Michael Camut

Does anyone really know what spirit is up to, or what inspiration is coming up next? From healing modalities, breathing techniques, now ministry. Being a reverend is a piece of a puzzle that fits neatly into my archetypes.

I know my journey on becoming a minister uncovered a bunch of hidden nuggets that were anxiously awaiting to be rediscovered. My relationship with shamanism was uncovered during a drumming session and is being pursued.

Holding space for others at their time of need, performing blessings, offering an ear for allowance to take its course, holding ceremonies for the expansion of love – all core ministry activities that will be predictably in my future.

Where I will be a year from now is not an easy one to predict. I know I will be continuing to expand just like during ministry school.

My guiding light is love and joy. Where I find and uncover these two gems, you know you will see my smiling face sharing and reflecting all of my love and joy right back.

Michael Camut

J. Sato

We are unique lights flickering in the Universe: sometimes brighter, higher, wider and fuller of grace. We are all beloved children of Source, Divine, Galaxies, God and as humans we inevitably trip and fall --discovering gunk that hinders our joy.

I seek to inspire, identifying paths to resonance with your personal relationship to the **benevolent something**, providing tools to discover and craft that special fingerprint to make ourselves and others better, happier, more love.

2020 has been an extraordinary year. May we continue to grow in flexibility, integrate and adapt to new conditions within our hearts and bodies, in our communities and on planet earth. Is there a better way to do this than to talk heart to heart, devotedly listen, remove the word "judgment" and together nourish a flourishing foundation? A genuine act of kindness may be as simple as a smile to a stranger **and** an authentic, continuous smile to **our** hearts.

Please join our Love Peace Harmony Meditation weekly at 7pm on Sundays. Details and Zoom link in CoM Newsletter and online in the calendar.

Peace to all.

J. Sato

Victoria Berends

I came to Circle of Miracles by way of a vivid dream and a friend's invite. I quickly found a place that was full of life-long seekers who welcomed all curious souls.

I went through the ministry program learning of concepts, self-discovery and changing in ways that may have taken my Self years, if not decades, to find on my own otherwise. I've been guided toward whatever path to my authentic self, my "I am", paves with Source.

This is a gift in circle's nature that I am thankful for helping me realize.

I can't presently name exactly what I'll be doing, and I may never know perfectly in advance, but I can now recognize a calling when it knocks. I can identify when to help, when to suggest, and when to release.

Whatever path forward arises within my internal guidance, or walks beside me in another way, will be where my ministry lies. I meet the world with the tools of love, hope, ease, and a willingness to be as I am. I plan to continue with my studies, while I remain open to opportunities of service, guided by Spirit, using my unique qualities, more of which I am yet to discover.

Thank you all for the support.

And so it is so.

Victoria Berends

4 - A Message From Hannelore

On the 15th Anniversary of Circle of Miracles, Rev. Hannelore gave a presentation on the journey that has since evolved into Circle of Circles.

What is Circle of Miracles?

Circle of Miracles is a Community that comes together to share with each other the many interesting ways we can walk the path Home - a place, A Course In Miracles says, we never really left.

"Do you know the best way home?" we ask each other, and some raise their hands claiming: "I think I know! I think I know!" What we don't know is that we were never lost. All paths lead Home, and we are just coming together to share, support, encourage, and love each other, helping to navigate the many possible ways.

The name implies Miracles. Indeed, Circle is built on a long string of Miracles: Circumstances that are orchestrated in another dimension and put into being in this one. At first glance, some of these circumstances seem to be disastrous, bad, or at least inconvenient. Our typical human reaction is: "NOW WHAT?" In retrospect, I know that they are always miraculous."

How did Circle and the Butterfly logo come to be?

"I, Hannelore, knew that every organization needs a logo. Playing with free clip art on the computer, I became intrigued by an image of a little boy, joyously riding on top of a butterfly, waving a bunch of flowers over his head. It spoke to my heart, to every cell of my body. It personified a joyous feeling of freedom. This is it! I made a few changes and let that became the perfect representation of Healing Alternatives. (Later on) I added two simple curved words over the little person waving the flowers: "Spirit Emerging"."

*Note: Earlier this year, the community voted on a new logo, which is on the cover of this booklet. Notice how there is a butterfly, a tribute to our roots and ever-evolving spirit.

The Miracle of the Mirror

(When Circle moved to Beulah Rd.)…"one suggestion was to place a huge six-foot round mirror on the wall. It was to have a one-foot frame, which we planned to decorate with icons of major world religions. Easier said than done! I searched the Internet with no results. One place in Philadelphia said they could create one. The problem would be the weight and how to suspend all that weight. Price? Over $1400 plus delivery and installation!

Now what?
Almost giving up, I happened to talk with one of Circle's graduate ministers, Phil and told him of our plight. He said, "NO PROBLEM!" and quickly created a lightweight six-foot round mirror with a one-foot frame. Exactly as planned. For FREE. Major MIRACLE! Another special friend of Circle, along with her husband, generously installed the mirror and placed rope lighting behind it, giving it a "floating" appearance.

Why a mirror, you ask? It reminds us that we are all mirrors for each other and that we are responsible for what we see "out there." Someone once said: "If you look into a mirror and see a spot on your face, you need to wipe your face." And A Course In Miracles states: "What you see reflects your thinking, and your thinking but reflects your choice of what you want to see." It is a beautiful teaching tool.

What I love best about this mirror was unintended by Phil, but turned out to be a little miracle: The mirror's surface is slightly curved, distorting the image a bit... perhaps reminding us that we don't see the real truth in ourselves and each other... yet.

Circle has been in existence for 15 years now: 12 years in Wycombe, 3 in New Britain. It has changed my life. Perhaps it has changed yours as well. I believe that Circle, like a pebble tossed into a pond, has birthed endless circles of miracles because of you, who carry the love and freedom you experience here into the world. I love each one of you!

Intense gratitude and unending blessings,"

Hannelore Goodwin

5 - A Note From Rev. Glenda Smith Director Circle of Miracles Ministries, Inc.

I would like to thank everyone who shared their stories about their experiences and connection with Circle. It was beautiful to read them all and know the feelings and experiences we all shared.

This book is the inspiration of Rev. Mike Wanner to document Circle's history. Thank you, Mike! To Rev. Sue Tweddale and Rev. Lisa Gidholm, thank you for your support and help in the editing process. It is a true work of Love.

As wonderful as it is to have the past 25 years recorded, it is the future that we must embrace. I feel confident it will be much different from the last 25 years. It is crucial, now more than ever, to fully embody the Divine beings that we are and realize how powerful we are. What we think and how we act is what we put out to the universe, and by cosmic law, the universe sends it back.

In our true essence, we are one with everything. We carry the same potential and the same Divine love that is the spark of all creation. We have the opportunity to see more clearly the world we want to create on Earth and assist with its evolution. To do that, we must be conscious of what we see "out there" and let go of anything standing in the way and blocking us from aligning and embodying the most vibrant possibilities - I Believe!

Please be sure to read the prayer "Declaration."

"I extend my hand and lovingly ask you to walk with me, in freedom, harmony, and peace."

Peace, Joy, and LOVE!

Glenda

6 - Circle Prayers

The founder wrote beautiful prayers that we still use.

Opening Prayer

I now ask the innermost center of my being
to release all negativity from the week just passed,
and throughout my life.
I let go of angry feelings and disturbing emotions.
I remove from my mind thoughts of doubt,
fear, guilt, and judgment.
I firmly discharge any beliefs of inadequacy,
ill health, or scarcity.
Beginning this very moment,
I allow myself to see the world as a possibility of
goodness, peace, and harmony.
I patiently look for good intentions, gentleness, and
cooperation.
I find evidence of health, forgiveness, joy, and
abundance.
I replace fear with love.
Because I sow strong, vigorous seeds of positive
expectations, carefully water and nourish them
by making an optimistic attitude part of my life,
the Divine Creative Force within me
grows a bountiful harvest from the very seeds I have
sown.
And so it is so!

Declaration

I am a Free Spiritual Being,
manifested from the Source of all life.
That is my true identity.
No person, place, or thing can hold power over me.
The unlimited wisdom and supply of my Source
is always flowing powerfully within me.
I choose to access this great Intelligence,
and live my life in harmony
with Its gentle, internal guidance.
Freedom is accepting my unique Self.
Freedom is letting go of my judgments,
and allowing others to affect their own destinies.
Freedom is lightheartedness,
and finding abundance everywhere.
Freedom is creating miracles with love, joy, and laughter.
Freedom is knowing that I really am Divine!
And, remembering who I am,
I extend my hand and lovingly ask you to walk with me,
in freedom, harmony, and peace.

Closing Prayer

Heavenly Creator, Divine Consciousness,
We welcome You into our awareness,
and open ourselves to Your loving guidance.
Awaken our direction in life
to the Universal Will of Your peaceful perfection.
We thank You for the blessings in our lives,
for seeing only our innocence.
Through Your presence in our hearts,
guide us in the light of Your Love,
in co-creation with the Divine Plan.
Amen

7 - Lovers Of Circle
Alphabetical by Last Name

Rev. Elaine Berk

Me & Circle

I'm not entirely sure how I found my way to Circle – but it certainly has been a beautiful gift in my life. I seem to vaguely remember one of my past life clients suggesting I might find like-minded, light-hearted individuals there. I believe it took me many months, possibly even a year, before I actually got myself to a Celebration, as with everything -- all in divine timing.

I clearly remember walking through the door and being welcomed; I remember feeling the vibration there and the loving energy emanating from a delightful petite powerhouse of a woman standing in the front of the room. I cannot recall much else about that day, but I knew I had found an exceptional place and that I would return.

Over time, Circle has become a home for me -- a soft place to land, an unconditional place to be, and a place I can always come and turn to, no matter what is transpiring in my life. I have learned, grown, expanded, and raised my vibration, and Circle has been an essential part of that.

I have shared Circle with friends, and I have made exceptional friends at Circle who have become family and dear loved ones.

I graduated from Circle's 2019 Ministry School class and continue my ministry; through and at Circle, and in the community at large.

It is important that Circle continues to thrive, offering a loving and meaningful presence in the community. As such, I have supported Circle in a variety of ways. I am honored to be a current Board member and help find ways to expand and bring Circle's unique gifts to the local community and now with Zoom, to all those who resonate with it, its services and programs.

Cheers and immense gratitude to Circle and all those involved – then, now, and to what it evolves into – always in the present moment.

Reverend Elaine Berk

November 15, 2020

Nicole Campbell

The path you have chosen is not an easy one. Alone, every moment is a mountain. Every thought becomes a compound sentence that spirals down—down.
Truth does not negate the difficulties, as it ought to do. No. It just illuminates the artistry in the energetic tangles you stumble upon.

But-together, you are strong, and strength becomes you.

A common cause motivates you to continue down your path. Every act of love is an outreached hand that keeps you balanced. step is an act of courage. Every slip is an opportunity Every to see things in a different light.
Page Break

Together every moment becomes an adventure. Every thought inspires you to build your wings and teach yourself how to fly.

This is why we gather. This is why.

Nicole Campbell

Michael Camut

Living and growing spiritually starts with belonging and participating with a loving community, a family, a place that you feel home with consciously and spiritually, a place where love lives and grows and is a part of each encounter and experience.

Living this lifetime with the omnipresence of Spirit, of God, allows us to continually grow and share our experiences. For me, as I first walked into Circle of Miracles, I connected with something bigger, something that gave me and still gives me an allowance to experience where I am presently while acknowledging my connection and yearning for expansion.

I had countless inner guidance and signs that all pointed me to expand my spirituality with the ministry school at Circle of Miracles. Attending this endeavor allowed me to look inward which in turn allowed me to look beyond myself. Experiencing points of views of other cultures, religions, and spiritualities, allowed me to grow and identify with the interfaith part of my ministry. The most rewarding was the inner work, the deep dive, the experiences of myself that were hidden and eager to be acknowledged.

Circle of Miracles is a place of allowance for one to experience their own unique path of spirituality and expansion. With my inner guiding light of love and joy, I offer a special blessing to all and especially to the Circle of Miracles community and wish a truly Happy 25th Anniversary. For I know that the next 25 years is going to be even more joyous and expansive.

Many Blessings,

Michael Camut

Rev. Jill Sabin Carel

As just one of the many individuals blessed by the existence of Circle of Miracles, I am eternally grateful for the tremendous impact that Ministry has had on my life. From the first time I attended a Circle service at the Wycombe home of Hannelore and Bob, I was entranced by the beauty and sacred space, Hannelore's awesome power in that little ageless body, Bob's folksy humor and intelligence, and the team of "angels" drawn to that Ministry.

The School of Ministry that graduated me in 2002 as an Interfaith Minister had an exemplary staff of instructors that rounded out my ministerial training. Many sacred gifts of Circle have been shared through my Ministry (before I retired) to have blessed many individuals through weddings, funerals, counseling, workshops, and my Self-Empowerment newsletter.

At Hannelore's memorial service, which I expected to be a somber occasion, I was astounded by the humor and huge outpouring of love for the superpower that she was! I have since moved to Florida and have recently enjoyed reconnecting on Sunday mornings via Zoom. The miracles keep flowing – 25 years and still going strong!

In eternal gratitude and love,

Rev. Jill Sabin Carel

Meera Carrol

Tribute to Hannelore and Bob

1996 was a very good year for me because I met Hannelore and Bob Goodwin at their fantastic home in Wycombe and attended Circle of Miracles for the first time in the fall.

Earlier that year, I attended the Olympics in Atlanta for ten days and came home to coordinate a Golf Outing at Cedarbrook Country Club the next morning at 9 AM. I was exhausted, and that day I fell and broke both my elbows. After a five-hour operation on my right elbow, I began my recovery.

Everyone was distraught for me. Even though it was painful, I was ecstatic to leave my corporate job with MCI after twelve years and retire. I prayed every day, chanted, and asked to be guided to find a spiritual community nearby.

Enter my neighbor, Mary Molle, and (my friend) Bernice Alterman (Harshida), who invited me to the Circle of Miracles. I followed them from Montgomeryville on a rollicking car ride trying to keep up with Mary and simultaneously write down the directions.

When I entered the energy room (Crystals were embedded under the floor, I was told), I say magnificent nature through the floor to ceiling glass windows. The exquisite spiritual energy awed me.

I felt unseen masters and spiritual teachers and Angels; a petite and beautiful Blond woman approached, and I felt an angelic presence. We instantly had a fantastic connection.

I also began studying the Course in Miracles in 1983 and was thrilled that the Circle of Miracles was based on the course. I loved the prayers, the music, and the table was laden with goodies. We couldn't stop eating the gourmet treats. YUM!

Hannelore was small but mighty - a powerful Capricorn who followed her inner guidance and had a fantastic work ethic. She was a leader who had studied and practiced many modalities and even went to India to study with Deepak Chopra. She could write a brilliant sermon and her strength was her intellect and especially her love and people skills. She knew everyone's strengths and loved us as one family, and encouraged us to participate. She created the ministry school while still teaching reiki classes, hypnosis, etc. At lunch, she would be working on her laptop as she munched.

I took Reiki I and Reiki 2 with Hannelore, and then in the summer, I retook Reiki 2. When Hannelore found out it was my birthday on 7/17, she disappeared and then returned with the cutest Teddy Bear wearing a sweater with an American flag on the front, and she announced this was my "Birthday Proxy." I was thrilled and immediately named him "Bearananda" and continue to use him to this day when I send Reiki. Hannelore and Bob were generous, kind, and like spiritual parents to us all.

A great blessing in my life was that a group of us went to Bob's nursing home and held his hand before he passed. Also, I got to be with Hannelore at Doylestown Hospital before she went into hospice. I can feel her presence at times and still feel her love and guidance. She chose a strong and amazing woman to continue her legacy, notably Rev. Glenda Smith, Director.

Yes, 1996 was an excellent year.

Rev. Sharon Cristofalo

COM has played an integral part in my spiritual growth with becoming an Interfaith Minister and enjoying beautiful friendships! COM has expanded my horizons and has allowed me to share my new found channeled gifts with LOVE.

Being part of Circle has continued to open my heart to embrace Unity with All, Oneness Consciousness, and accept everyone and everything without judgment. I love how we each at Circle are bright twinkling stars, each unique and with different perspectives, allowing others to shine too.

I am grateful for COM and all my COM friends.

Happy 25th!

Many Blessings for another 25!!!!

Rev. Sharon Cristofalo, MA, PT

Rev. Susan Delorenzo

The Invitation

My first encounter with Hannelore Goodwin took place in 1998. We moved to Bucks County from Waukesha, WI, because of my husband's work. As I was walking through Newtown, I noticed an "angel store" and popped in. The store was quiet; the owner and I were the only ones present; we spent time together chatting about our spiritual journeys. She suggested I go to Wycombe to participate in a Reiki share at Hannelore Goodwin's home; I did and went every Wednesday evening. A feeling of love, peace, and gratitude filled me as I connected with those present sharing this beautiful gift of Reiki. While I was there, I heard people talking about the Sunday morning gathering, mmm interesting. My husband and I had been very active in our church throughout our marriage, so I felt hesitant to attend.

One Sunday morning, after meditating, I felt a strong nudge to go to Wycombe for the gathering. I listened, jumped out of bed, quickly dressed, etc. to attend my first Sunday gathering in Wycombe. My husband asked, "where are you going"? I responded, "I don't know, a meeting"? The only thing I knew for sure was that my soul was very persistent that I attend. I walked in, not knowing what to expect, and, after being there for two hours, I knew why my soul was so insistent. The prayers, the music, the speakers/sparks, and the meditation filled me, and I knew I had found my new spiritual community.

Every Saturday evening, I felt an excitement just thinking about being at Circle the following morning! The community was welcoming; the dialogue after the speaker/spark helped me get to know them as they shared their comments, what had come up for them as they listened. I was home. Bucks County had welcomed me with open arms. I fell in love with love.

I have surprised myself by taking on leadership roles here at Circle; being a Board President was not in my realm of thinking. But I heard the "voice" asking and telling me it was time to give back, to step out of my comfort zone, and serve the community I so loved and valued. I also hear "Hannelore's" voice now and again telling me to hang in there, keep embracing, keep listening to the call.

So many memories, so many changes, so much love.

So, here I am 22 years later, still growing, still appreciating, always loving, what a Gift Circle has been for me. I cherish the friendships I have made in my years here at Circle and feel an inner excitement for those I have yet to meet. Some dear friends have transitioned, and they will forever hold a sweet place in my heart. What a blessing you have all been; I am grateful.

Patricia Gallagher

This article appeared in The Chestnut Hill Local newspaper - 2014

Editors note: Trisha founded The Happy Flower Day Project last year with the help of Bob and Hannelore Goodwin, who are both ministers at the Circle of Miracles Church in New Britain, PA. Tricia, who puts 100 miles on her car on an average day, picks up day-old flowers from grocery stores that would otherwise be thrown away, and she delivers them to nursing homes and hospitals all over the area to cheer up patients. In many cases, the flowers have a therapeutic effect.

Patricia's story was titled - 'Heart' of a 91-year-old man is an inspiration - 'Random acts of flowering' cheering up elderly patients.

My mother, Claire Mohan, passed away on April 22 of this year in at-home hospice at age 88. Until the end, she would help me deliver the flowers because it gave her life a purpose, which was to brighten the patients' days. She could not go in most of the time with me (but in the beginning six months she could), but she waited in the car while I ran in and did my thing.

Another man, Bob, who was 91 on July 23 of this year, also helped me deliver flowers. He lives in an assisted living place now, The Solana on Horsham Road in North Wales, and his health is failing. His spirits are pretty low these days. We had a lot of good times being the Flower People. He needed a purpose for living, too, which was fulfilled by the flower deliveries. I loved listening to Bob's stories about going to Yale University, being a Navy officer, and his career with U.S. Steel. I think the story about these good people who have come along for the ride is very uplifting.

Bob, who inspires me, and I would start our flower caper adventure with a jolt of coffee from McDonald's and a cinnamon bun. He often brought his harmonica along and played a tune as I passed out the flowers. I call these deliveries "random acts of blooming smiles." Every morning I send a silent prayer towards the heavens and ask, "God, who needs the gift of a beautiful bouquet today?"

My internal God GPS device leads me to half-way houses, AIDS hospices, nursing homes, and even random bus stops and train stations. In 14 months, I have had the privilege of being the deliverer of 19,451 bouquets of fresh flowers. Most days, I have close to a hundred bouquets to pass out to strangers.

Yesterday, I went to The Solana assisted living facility in North Wales and walked into the dining room. The staff and residents know me because I stop by about once a month. I was there to pass out flowers and to visit my friend Bob. Before he was hospitalized last December, he was my helper in flower deliveries. Now at age 91, Bob had a concern that was more pressing than others. He looked at me intently. "Trish, it looks like I am going to be living here permanently. My wife is also going through serious health issues. I can't think of any words that can comfort her. I need care now, also. It is too much for

48

her to have to worry about me while she is trying to heal. I don't know what is wrong with my legs, and I have to use oxygen some of the time."

I asked him, "Bob, what is that orange pouch hanging on your wrist?" He said, "Trish, that is my crystal heart in there. It is just a felt bag, and it symbolically holds my wife's heart. Every morning and night, I take the crystal heart out of the holder and use it and send my love to her.

"I 'Reiki' the heart. I ask God to have my love touch her in the way that my words cannot right now. I motion my fingers over it. I used to hang it on my walker. I didn't want to lose it or forget to pray on it. So now I keep it on my wrist. I can't lose it at night if it is on my wrist. It is with me when I am in bed."

I said, "Bob, that is the most loving thing I have ever heard. So many people are separated from loved ones. In recovery houses, prisons, overseas serving our country or in hospitals and nursing homes."

I thought of my dear mother, who passed away on April 22. The three of us used to go to the Piano Bar restaurant sing-a-long on Tuesday nights. Then their health declined at about the same time. Bob always sang patriotic songs, and my mother sang her favorite Patsy Cline tunes.

"Bob, what a great idea!" I said. "I am going to buy a heart and 'talk' to my mother in heaven, too. Let's tell other people about it. What do you want to call it?"

"Oh geez, Trish. 'Hearts Away 'is what comes to my mind right now. Sort of like when I was serving in the Navy in the Philippines. We used to say 'Anchors Away.' I have her heart with me all of the time. My real heart is never away from her."

We are older, and we can't do this kind of travel. We want to live this travel dream vicariously through you.

I went there and got my "groove back." For a whole month, I smiled, laughed, practiced Spanish, went on long bus rides that only cost 25 cents, enjoyed two dollar meals at great restaurants, volunteered at an orphanage, and even bought an antibiotic prescription for three dollars at a pharmacy. And they gave me the medicine without even seeing a doctor. I survived without access to a computer or phone!

I felt like a teenager again – carefree! Not a care in the world. It was just what I needed. I didn't know what I needed at the time, but the Universe and the "Miracle Workers" at Circle of Miracles sure did!

Jennifer Goodwin

I met Hannelore when I took her Reiki I Class at Holy Family College in Northeast Philadelphia in January 1999 and joined Circle of Miracles immediately thereafter. Though the time I spent there before moving away was relatively short, the connection to Circle was permanent.

I am so thrilled that the virtual celebrations of 2020 have allowed me to reconnect with my spiritual home all these years later.

Thank you to all, and congratulations on 25 years!

With love and gratitude,
Jennifer Goodwin *(no relation to Bob and Hannelore)

Sam Haines

My favorite story about the Circle of Miracles

"My first encounter with COM was back in 2010. I was performing music as part of a fund-raising event for Susie Beiler. I had only recently connected with people who are now dear and life-long friends. I have since played music for COM many times and have been a guest speaker two times. The most notable moment for me at Circle was on that day, preparing to perform for the fundraiser in 2011. I clearly remember walking in and seeing Wendi Rose for the first time. It was one of those magic moments where the whole room disappeared, and I saw only her. I do not remember having any more contact than a brief introduction from a friend, and I moved along into my activities to get ready to perform music.

In the years since that first meeting, Wendi and I have come to recognize each other as beloveds with a shared mission of helping people to connect with the heart of their soul and live an empowered journey here on earth.

Without Circle of Miracles and the unique community that has gathered around its mission, I am sure Wendi and I would have met, and these precious friends would be in my life, but a precious hearthstone would be missing from my life. Circle of Miracles will always be a place of warmth, light in the darkness, and a piece of home."

And you can quote me on that! Sam Haines

Alison Kritzer

Congratulations, Circle of Miracles, on your 25th Anniversary!

You bring such Light to Bucks County!!! So many of us wouldn't be here without you. We would not – could not – do what we do if not for you. You've been a steady, loving presence all these years. Always there, always holding the torch for us. You guide us, encourage us, show us by example.

Most importantly, you foster and support us. You come to the expos, host the events & classes, and celebrate with us. You lead with love - smiling, encouraging, guiding.

Circle of Miracles - Bucks County, Pennsylvania, The United States, The World, and The Universe would be very different places without you.

I'm so glad you're here!

Alison Kritzer
www.PranicHealingBucksCounty.com

Annette Kroninger

The Miracle of how I came to COM?

In 1996 I was feeling that I really didn't belong anywhere and felt lost and alone. I was married for the 2nd time, had two grown children, a teaching career and a nice house, but I felt lonely in my world. I was looking to get involved in something meaningful and fulfilling.

I had enjoyed going to psychic intuitive readers throughout my adult life and found myself going to Shadow Wolf, a Shaman psychic who was giving readings in a Spiritual shop in Doylestown. I don't remember much of what was said in that reading except that near the end of the reading, she said I would be getting connected or involved with elephant energy. I had no idea what that meant, thinking I was going to have to visit the Zoo. She was certain that this energy would attract me in some way within the next few months. I left thinking that was a bizarre reading.

Soon after that reading, I decided to sign up for a "Day for All Women" retreat at Bucks County Community College out of curiosity. I was supposed to go with two friends who both backed out of the event. I still went feeling driven to be there and that it would be important for me to be there. Before the event I had registered for a sequence of speakers, but when I got there, I became spontaneous and changed my list and went to speakers and topics that were quite different. I went to a

Dream Interpretation workshop led by Ute Arnold first. Then I went to an Introduction to Reiki given by Hannelore Goodwin. I had no idea what Reiki was, but it sounded interesting. I later found out that Ute and Hannelore were good friends.

Hannelore described Reiki and came around giving us a sample of Reiki Energy on our shoulders. I liked the relaxing Reiki energy and wanted to learn more about it, so I signed up for Reiki Level 1 with Hannelore Goodwin which was being taught at her home in Wycombe.

I went to her class and felt very relaxed and comfortable with Reiki. During our lunch break, I went into her office and looked up and saw a whole shelf of elephants. I asked Hannelore why she had this collection of elephants and she said that was her energy, Elephant Energy.

At that moment I remembered what Shadow Wolf had said in the reading a few months before and immediately got goosebumps on my arms. I knew I was supposed to be with Hannelore learning Reiki and whatever I could. I continued from then on to take classes from Hannelore and attend the COM Sunday Services and eventually graduate from Ministry School.

I have always felt like I had found my way back to my Spiritual Home and Family which was what I desired my whole life. I remember who I am and feel like I can be the real me when I am at COM. It is my place to reconnect with my spiritual Self and other like-minded souls traveling this path together. My life has changed so much from my connection to Circle of Miracles. I am filled with Gratitude for Circle of Miracles.

Many years later, I have really come to appreciate the synchronicity and connection of all the perfect opportunities that came together to guide me to Hannelore Goodwin, Circle of Miracles and Reiki.

Annette Kroninger

Debbra Lupien

Congratulations on your 25th Anniversary, Circle of Miracles!

It was a great honor to be welcomed into the Circle family as a guest Speaker. The graciousness and generosity of spirit I experienced at Circle of Miracles was reminiscent of a Divine embrace.

Through determination, intention, positive energy, and love, you've created an extraordinary community. May you continue as a shining beacon awakening souls for many years to come.

Debbra Lupien, Voice of the Akashic Records

answers@akashaunleashed.com*

Marcy McGuire

HOW I DISCOVERED CIRCLE OF MIRACLES

It took a while, but I finally got here!

It was the early 2000's, and each Spring and Fall, the Central Bucks School District Continuing Education brochure arrived in my mailbox, filled with a wide selection of exciting classes and workshops. One particular course for personal development, "Reiki Level 1" sounded intriguing, taught by Hannelore Z. Goodwin, a name hard to forget. I must have googled "Reiki" but not been too sure what it was all about, so did not sign up. I wasn't quite "there" yet if you know what I mean.

Fast forward to 2007, the class offered through (a friend of Circle's) Susan Duval's newsletter landed me in a weekend of Psych-K Training, paired up with Mary Scheets, R.N. I did not know at the time that Mary was (or was soon to be) an ordained Reverend through the ministry school established by Hannelore Z. Goodwin at Circle. (Spirit has such a sense of humor and a marvelous, although often roundabout, way of getting things done!)

When spring 2009 continuing education brochure arrived, there was that "Reiki Level 1" class again, but this time the teacher was listed as Mary Scheets, R.N. Wow, I remembered her! What a coincidence. (Oh, really???) Time to sign up.

Being attuned to Reiki was a life changer for me. As Level 1 was wrapping up, Mary suggested that her students practice Reiki by attending Tuesday evening Reiki Share at Circle of Miracles, facilitated by Rev. Glenda Smith. So, I followed up and discovered Circle and all it has to offer.

There I met a wonderful, diverse group of talented, friendly people; kindred spirits on the quest. We've shared the energy, the music, the love (the potluck food!), and have witnessed each others' spiritual journeys.

I will always remember the wintry Tuesday evening that Hannelore made an unannounced appearance at Reiki Share. I was thrilled to meet her. After many years of seeing her name in that brochure, she was now a part of my Reiki lineage.

I happily acknowledge that my journey to Circle would not have been possible without the Central Bucks School District Continuing Education brochures. Spirit's subtle but persistent nudges, Susan Duval, Mary Scheets, Rev. Glenda Smith and Hannelore Z. Goodwin, and that I found a spiritual home at Circle of Miracles through the lovely gift of Reiki.

Marcy McGuire

Marcy's Other Fond Memories of Circle:

The dedication and creativity of Circle's leadership and volunteers - thank you all!

The inspiring and passionate speakers for Sunday Celebration

The joyful guitar playing and singing by Rev. Annabella Wood

Musical offerings by Neo, David Young, Sam Haines, Eric Labacz, Rev. Sharon Kachel

Bob Goodwin's Sunday Celebration "Seeds"

Hannelore's explanation of the many-faceted crystal star candleholder & her fashionable shoe   collection

New Year's Eve Reiki Share and Kirtan

Patricia Gallagher's delightful talks - the "Flower Lady."

Solstice & Equinox Reiki Share potlucks with LIVE music - thank you, Glenda!!!

Taking photos of orbs at one of Gene Ang's workshops

Seeing photos of orbs over the students at Lynda & Annette's children's Reiki class

Getting "didged" (didgeridoo sound bath) by Harold E. Smith

Always feeling welcome

Marcy

Carol Morotti-Meeker

Circle of Miracles is a group of mostly spiritual or heading in that direction in their way; people who don't have much dogma and come from spirit. My late friend Tom Osher got me to go.

I have had some great times there in services and more fun activities, which helped speed me on my journey while touching me in the heart. Many of the people I have met follow what Neil Diamond sang about in "Brother Love's Salvation Show" - one hand to spirit and the other out to your fellow human. Isn't that what the sacred community is supposed to be? It is in my book.

COM, On to another 25 years.

Best,

Carol Morotti-Meeker
Alchemist of the Divine Feminine

Peter Moses

Always in my heart, I carry a vision of Hannelore Goodwin glowing as she welcomes a Sunday Celebration. The unconditional love, the felt sense of inclusion and oneness shines brightly, as it is reflected by all in attendance. I can see and hear her husband Bob, with his warm voice and sense of humor, as he delivers some Spiritual Seeds. There is laughter. There are tears.

There is love. Plus, in the timeless tradition of Circle of Miracles, there is an abundance of hugs!

One of the 'miracles' of Circle is that, within every gathering of souls there, people seem to receive the exact gifts of clarity and affirmation that are most vital for them. It is a great joy to speak, sing, play, share and listen in the open arms and ears of Circle.

The "future" of Circle is unfolding NOW as every day, the thousands of human beings touched deeply by Circle are spreading the Light of Consciousness to everyone they meet. Of Course, the timing is perfect. Thank God! And it is equally true to say THANK YOU

Peter Moses

Rev. Wendi Rose

Wendi's Story .

My first encounter with the Circle of Miracles and Hannelore was back in 1996. I was looking for a Reiki teacher. She invited me to one of her Reiki shares. I loved it!

Then she invited me to a Sunday Celebration. It was my first time being around a group of loving, accepting, and open-hearted spiritual people. When everyone holds hands, shares miracles, and sings at the end of the service, let there be peace on earth, an overwhelming feeling of love and blessings burst through me. I could not hold back my tears of joy that shook my entire body. Both Hannelore and Bob held me so tight and did not let go until I was complete. I was home.

Wendi's Story 2

The unique nickname that Hannelore gave me was "Puppy" Why did she give me this name; you may be thinking. It was an evening at one of Hannelore's reiki shares. It was a full house— at least five people to 3 tables. I was a bit anxious that evening, so I participated for a bit and then went to Hannelore's office, where she was busy on her computer. At this time, they had just gotten a new puppy named Misha. He was sleeping peacefully next to Hannelore. All I wanted to do was move this anxious energy out of me, so the best thing I thought of was getting down on the floor with Misha and becoming a puppy. We rolled around on the floor and played like puppies. It was so much fun. Misha could not contain his excited energy, so the moment the door opened to the reiki share room, Misha ran as fast as he could around each table, and no one could stop him.

What was a quiet reiki healing space became a loud space that was full of laughter.

I became one with the spirit of puppy energy that evening. To Hannelore, I will always be her puppy!

Favorite Hannelore Quote: "Oh my healing back" was the words I heard Hannelore say when she had back pain.

Reverend Anne Scull

Circle of Miracles
Most of my involvement with COM (spanning over at least ten years) revolved around the Ministry School. Hannelore, the instructors, and the students were among the most excellent spiritual guides I have encountered. Besides the introduction to A Course in Miracles, Reiki, various World Religions, and how to perform Rituals, here are just a few of the take-aways that remain relevant - and a foundation for - my current spiritual life.

- There is no "other."

- Everything in life is either an act of love or a call for love.

- When I experience someone/something in life as irritating, I examine myself to see how that same quality is present in my thoughts/actions and reflect on how I can grow from the experience.

- The greatest prayer is the prayer of gratitude.

- I am a unique expression of God.

- I "miss the mark" when I believe in separation.

- Body awareness leads to Soul awareness.

- Chocolate solves all problems. :>)

I could go on and on. Thank you, COM! Rev. Anne Scull

Rev. Glenda Smith

I clearly remember the first time I walked into Circle. It was around 1997-1998. I had done a few Unergi sessions with Ute' Arnold, and she told me about this beautiful place she went to every Sunday and invited me to join her. When I called her a few weeks later, she was not going that Sunday and encouraged me to go without her. When she gave me the address, my reaction was, "Wycombe? Where is that?" I had moved here in 1989 from Massachusetts and had never heard of Wycombe! However, being a yard sale enthusiast, I got out my maps and planned a route. (This was in the years before GPS.)

I found it, and little did I know how it would change my life! When I walked in, I felt something, which, at the time, I had no explanation. It felt good, excellent. I didn't have time to think about it as several people immediately warmly welcomed me, and the "service" began. I had explored many religions and attended many different Sunday services but never found anything I could believe in wholeheartedly. This seemed different, "maybe…", I thought. I kept going back and never had to search again. Except deep inside!

In 1999 when Hannelore announced that Circle would start a Ministry School, I immediately knew I wanted to attend. I also knew the company I had moved here for was closing, and I was going to be unemployed, AND I had just bought my first home. There was "no way" I could afford to attend. The first night of class came and went, and I called Hannelore in tears and said,

"I don't know how I can pay for it, but "I KNOW I'M SUPPOSED TO BE THERE." I remember it clearly because that was not something I usually said. (I am getting emotional writing this.) She told me to come and pay as I could. When I finally was laid off, I went to auctions and yard sales and resold at flea markets. I quickly delivered the tuition to be ordained and graduate with the first class in 2001. I had never heard of metaphysics and healing energies like Reiki and could not learn fast enough!

I took Master Teacher Reiki as soon as it was offered after Ordination and started the Reiki Share, which now meets at Circle, in my home, and began to teach some Reiki class. That was 18 years ago, and I still look forward to Reiki share night each week. I even found a way to continue on Zoom during the pandemic.

After Ordination I stayed very active with Hannelore, the ministry school, and all things Circle. One day Hannelore called me at my job and asked if I had a few minutes to talk. I did and was shocked when she asked if I would like to be Co-Director of Circle Sunday Celebrations with her! I did not even have to think about it. "YES!" was my immediate reply. It was around 2008. When Circle moved out of Wycombe to New Britain, I also became Co-Director of the Ministry School. Hannelore and I did some co-teaching of Reiki Classes, and I began to teach Reiki regularly at Bucks County Community College and eventually at Circle.

Over the years, the Ministry School evolved. I loved working on new curriculums with Hannelore, Rev. Mother Jo Ellen Werthman, and her husband, Rev. Rob Werthman. Rev. Laura Barry, and Rev. Anne Scull. In the last couple of years, the Ministry School has evolved again. It has been exciting working with Rev. Rhian Lockard and Rev. Susan McCashew to see a successful new program coming to fruition.

One of the things I was instrumental in was developing new programming and instituting the website calendar and newsletter. These things, too, continue to evolve, and I look forward to seeing what the next 25 years will bring!!!

Happy Anniversary and Love to all!!!

Lauren Thomas

After relocating eight years ago from New Jersey, where I was blessed to be among a like-minded group of metaphysical friends, I now felt a little lost.

The day that I walked into Circle of Miracles, I knew right away that I had found my new spiritual home.

How wonderful to be in the loving energy of this sacred space. Learning and exploring the universal truths of who we are, without judgment or fixing, is Miracle!

Thank you, my Circle family, for the opportunity to be among you to share in praying and growing while we hold the space for each other.

A little bit of Heaven on Earth!

Rev. Sue Tweddale

I was 25 years old, just starting a corporate career and taking on the world as an adult. I wasn't sure what I believed spiritually, but I sensed that there was something more than what religion taught. I paid no mind, always deciding I'd get back to that curiosity later in life. But then, my mom was diagnosed with ovarian cancer and was struggling for her life.

The first time I heard the Voice of Spirit was in the waiting room following my mom's surgery. The voice was gentle and calm, but insistent. "You HAVE to get in to see your mother." This "voice" had a momentum to it and took over my body as I watched from the back of my mind. I found myself asking, then convincing the doctor to let me into the recovery room. He did. That was the first Miracle. (it was 1987, and hospitals did not allow that yet).

As I stood next to her bed in the recovery room, the voice said: "You need to touch her." I found a spot on her forehead and placed my hand there. I looked down at her lovingly, and I remember thinking that I wished I could give her my strength. All of a sudden, I felt energy flow from me to her. At that time, I had no point of reference whatsoever to explain this. I was blown away and knew from that moment that I could never again doubt that there is more to this world, and it involved some unseen benevolent force.

Fast forward to the year 1999. My cousin tells me about this spiritual community she found where they teach Reiki. She said it sounded like it might explain what occurred with my mom. I took Reiki Level I and met Hannelore. When I met her, I felt that same sense of calm I experienced when I heard that voice. When I walked into the Energy Room at Wycombe, it felt like home. I went on to meet a wonderful circle of like-minded souls, where I finally felt seen wholly and entirely understood in my expression of open-minded spirituality and oneness.

I went on to become a Reiki Master Teacher and graduated from the ministry school in November 2001 and have remained actively involved behind the scenes ever since.

The Circle of Miracles was the catalyst for a significant change in my life. There were growing pains along the way. Navigating through the ministry program involved a deep inner dive in discovering the true Self by owning the negative and nurturing the positive, leading to ultimate love and acceptance of Self. That was all part of becoming a "real" girl. Here's what happened as a result of finding my spiritual home and my true Self:

- got a divorce. It was hard but the right choice. My ex is happily remarried, as am I.

- met my current husband at Circle.

- "manifested" a layoff from my corporate job, which was no longer healthy for me.

- became a massage therapist, giving Reiki to others regularly

- opened and owned my own massage business for four years.

I have heard numerous stories from others at Circle who stepped fully into their lives due to connecting with the Circle community. Miracles abound every day, and I am eternally grateful for all who have blessed my life.

Evelyn Wanner

My feelings about the Circle of Miracles

I love the people and the service. When I 1st heard "Be Welcome Here," I fell in love. The song changed so many things for me.

The thing I love the most is the three prayers. I think they are life-changing IF you say them every day.

Circle gets such fabulous speakers. Services are always a learning process.

Annabella was the music minister when I first started coming, and I loved her songs and voice. So, I would hear her, and I was so blessed to be there at that time.

Thank God for this beautiful place of worship.

Congratulations

Evelyn Wanner

Rev. Mike Wanner

I met Hannelore in 1993 and was impressed with her Reiki share and then her and then all that was to be. I had a great experience throughout this time and enjoy the peace, presence, and opportunities that she and eventually her Ministry and now the Circle community offers.

It is such a supportive community of like-minded people who are so very open to sharing and living and loving all that Creator offers us all. The Joy of Circle of Miracles is palpable and inviting to all who cross the threshold or zoom to our celebrations, workshops, and events.

The International Metaphysical Ministry already ordained me before coming to Circle of Miracles Ministry School, and each Institution contributed significantly to the peace within me. Both offered the depth of academic education and a massive expansion of Spiritual alignment, focusing on personal understanding and empowerment.

Circle of Miracles offers the vibrancy of personal meetings and workshops that simplify the alignment with the Divine by step by step week by week expansion into the Joy of Aligning with the Divine while having a great time

The Circle of Miracles Community is a fantastic group of people who bring unique talents and skills to share for the betterment of us all.

The Ministry school at Circle of Miracles has graduated over 150 ministers over the years. A key component in that Training is self-care that allows each student minister to take charge of their life and optimize it.

Every student minister seems to bring gifts for Circle, the greater community, and the world. Supporting each other raises the Circle Community's ability to nurture the earth and its people.

Peace, Love, and Healing is core to our service to the world, and I am proud of all we have done already and what is to come.

Thanks for the blessings that I have received by being part of Circle. Congratulations to us all, AND SO IT IS!

Rev. Mike Wanner

Rev. Edie Weinstein

I walked through the door of Hannelore and Bob Goodwin's haven in the woods that was the initial location for Circle of Miracles and felt as if I had come home. I was invited by Peter Moses who sensed that I belonged there. That was in 2001 and now 19 years later, I am certain that I do. The people, the inspiration, the music, the love, and the hugs kept me coming back. Hannelore and Bob were not only my friends but a surrogate mom and dad after mine passed.

In October, I received this timely message from Hannelore via her daughter Teri. Although it came to me, it was clearly meant to be shared with the world as we attempt to sort through a myriad of emotions in the time of COVID-19 and political unrest.

"Sweet, dear, golden-hearted Edie. We see your struggle to make sense of all the happenings. You fight bravely to understand the events and other people's complacency, or outright agreement with the events. You feel the pull to save those who are entranced by the narcissistic energy vortex. Your courage to confront and be a clearing for difficult conversations is one of your deepest strengths. Thank you for standing for the light.

We are here to ask you to put this load down. We have this. You are becoming exhausted. Your focus is fuzzy. Your concentration is off. We see you. We hear you. We send love and this message: those you are now speaking to cannot be reached unless they want to be reached.

They cannot be "woken up" by you. This is their journey. This is hard for you. You embrace transformation and wonder why others don't. Let them sleep. It is their choice. Instead, determined warrior, we ask that you turn your energy and focus inward. Not in the way of an "ostrich." No. Rather, when you turn inward, you will have access to a whole new powerful set of tools that lie within you. Your ability to work with energy and transform it is very much needed now.

We are in the "vise" between two competing, divergent energies on the planet. Because you care for this world on a soul level, you have felt at a loss for something "to do." You have become distraught from this love of the world. We hear you. We ask you to consider these ongoing, daily actions to help transform the energy pattern on this planet.

WITNESS: do not turn away from world events, rather be a witness without resistance. This is not the same as ignoring events. We ask you to be aware and witness because resistance, especially in the form of judgement, reinforces the low vibrational energies. But witnessing is the first step to transforming the energies. Notice/witness everything unfolding and... allow.
ALLOW: Notice when your judgement arises (and it will). This is an opportunity to transform that energy from low vibration to spirit vibration within yourself. Allowing means that you witness whatever-you-are-judging to "be" (without judgement). Also, as your judgements arise be kind to yourself. Be as gentle with yourself as you are with others. Your kindness must be turned inward too. Just witness and allow, beloved one.

TRANSFORM : include energetic hygiene practices daily. The energies that swirl around now are intense, dark and overwhelming at times, for they are fighting for existence. When you spend energy to clear YOUR vessel (align chakras daily, meditate, ask for angel help, ask for angel/spirit messages) you become a tool for the light. You create the ability to send all witnessed energies through to another plane. You live in the physical plane. We (angels/spirits and loved ones) do not. We actually cannot do this work without you. WE NEED YOU.

Self-care and energy hygiene are of the utmost importance. (They are repeating this to make sure you understand: Energy used to "change" those who sleep, has no impact beyond exhausting you.)

When your vessel is clear you become a walking conduit of witness-allow-transform. To send energies to the other plane, you must simply ask. "Take this and transform this. Thank you."

Final message: Edie, you are here because you chose this opportunity to transform the world. This has called you all your life, and indeed you have transformed many lives. THIS is the moment you have prepared for. You will transform by your heart witnessing the world, allowing it and passing it through. You are being called to be. You are loved. You are safe. We are with you.

Hannelore add- on: Be at peace Edie. I am in the music you chose. I am alongside you when you call. Put your burden down. Let it pass to us. I love your soul deeply and wish to reach out, but it's hard for me to get through the "world pain" you carry. Namaste communicator. I wait for your channel to clear and am always there."

Rev. Annabella Wood

I came to PA as part of a result of an upsetting divorce in CA. I had been active in the spiritual community back there, and because of the divorce, I was challenging all the spiritual "truths" in my belief system. None of it was feeling very real at the time. Upon arriving here, I met an old friend from CA who would be speaking at the Circle of Miracles and thought I might enjoy going with her. So I went. It was at Bob and Hannelore's house in Wycombe. I brought my guitar as my friend wanted me to play some of my original music to back up her talk. We arrived, and I put the guitar in the stand, off to the side where I could reach it. We had a good service, and I sang my songs, but my heart wasn't in it. I felt that I had a long journey ahead of me without the spiritual community. I preferred anonymity. I didn't want to be known. But there was a feeling that when I returned to what I knew was right, I would return here. Now was not the time. I couldn't pretend that any of this was working for me. So I left their house after service, not knowing how long it would be before I returned. But when I left, my guitar stand remained behind.

Hannelore called to let me know I had left my guitar stand. I thanked her and said I would come one Sunday and get it. Time went by. Maybe a year. I heard from Hannelore again. I still wasn't ready but just told her to hang on to it. I would get it eventually. They moved to New Britain, and Hannelore called with the new address. Still, I wouldn't come.

Then one day, I was ready. I just woke up on a Sunday and knew I was prepared to stop grieving and begin healing. I would be going to the Circle of Miracles to perform a miracle on my own heart. I walked into the room, and there was beautiful Hannelore. I didn't expect her to know who I was, but she took one look at me and smiled so brightly. I guess she did that with everyone, but I felt it was just for me. I felt so welcomed and unworthy, as it had been many years. How did she recognize me? But she did. I felt so welcomed that I just started to cry as she gave me her signature hug. I was finally home to heal.

She took my hand and walked me toward the front of the room. There on the right side, as if it belonged there, was my old guitar stand. I put my guitar in the stand and proceeded to play original music in the beautiful Sunday Celebration for about ten years.

The circle continues to be a welcoming, healing community. I will never forget how spirit never let me get too far away by using a homing beacon in the form of a guitar stand.

Rev. Annabella Wood

Ruth Anne Wood

Circle Talk Inspired Art

The Sunday guest presenter speaks with intimate, loving, angelically guided messages.

My pen races to keep up on the Circle program as I immediately recognize the details being said about a long-time friend I had met at Pebble Hill Church in my early teens in the late 1980s. I fondly recall this brilliantly, smiling, white-haired, retired gentleman doing ballet and Shakespearean performances in the park. During this channeled talk, Jim Kotch sits beaming in a row behind me.

As I listen to Cheryl Blumenthal address this stranger by the first name, I immediately see a Karen Hoffman style watercolor form in my mind's eye. After the service, I boldly ask Karen, this beloved artist, to co-create the talk's inspired piece in her studio.

After having to reschedule our artist date, I am driving up to Karen and Herk's lush Wycombe forest to an inspiring custom homemade from the trees on the land. It's just walking distance from Bob and Hannelore's first Circle Of Miracles home.

After taking in the forest air, sitting on the patio for lunch, Karen shows me her studio whose art adorns their beautiful home.

Karen paints her classic Circle, and then we let spirit guide us as we play in the center. I make a rainbow handprint and glue on a paper that reminds me of Jim after cutting it out. As I add Cheryl's words in pencil around the Circle, Karen's whimsical paint strokes dance on the page.

Little do we know at that very moment that Karen and I are honoring Jim, Hannelore, and friends are treating Jim Kotch to lunch on his 88th birthday! #DivineTiming.

Jim feels so honored by the piece, he insists on treating me and my husband Jason to a fancy dinner at William Penn Inn.

Just like my beloved friends, I have many Circle stories of the synchronicities and Spirit-guided connections.

With a hand to your heart, honor the beloved Circle family who you've cherished over the years. Breathe deeply, remembering the incredible healing sensations of the Circle community gathered in sacred space.

-Ruth Anne Wood, Scripting For Success

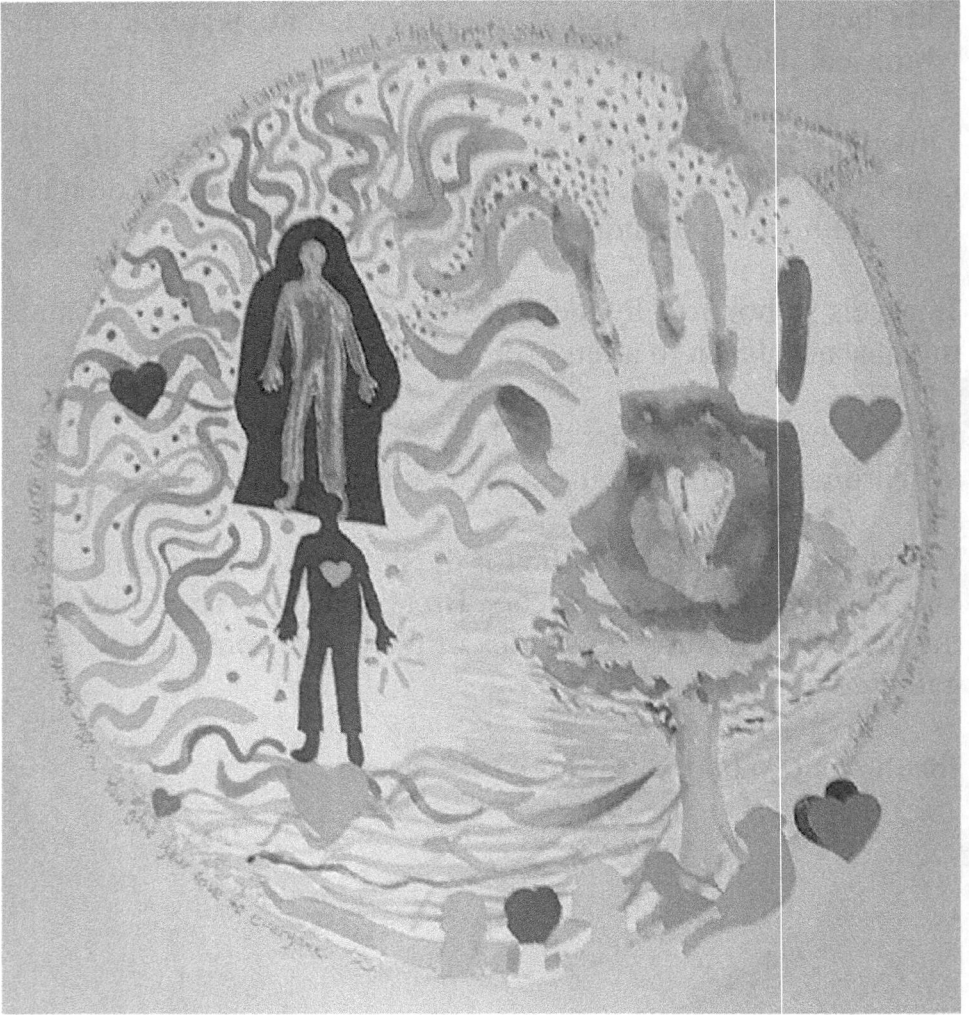

Jim Kotch's painting now resides in Ruth's office.

8 - Special Recognition

Rev Glenda Smith has been a steady anchor here at COM. When Circle found it's new home in New Britain, Glenda joined Hannelore as co-director. She had been holding services in her home for a few years prior to the move from Wycombe to New Britain. I had attended a few circle services in Lansdale, Glenda's home, and was pleased to know that she and Hannelore would be co-facilitating our Sunday Celebrations.

Hannelore transitioned in 2015. On July 25th, I, along with Rev. Glenda, Rev. Laura Barry, and Rev. Anne Skull facilitated a Life Celebration for Hannelore, it was quite an honor to be a part of this Celebration for our friend.

At this celebration I witnessed Glenda step into her own shoes, and felt a heart smile along with a knowing, that we would be gently guided into a new wave at COM with Glenda taking the reigns as our Director.

Her dedication to Circle and the community was present as we went through the many changes suggested by members of Hannelore's family and the Circle guardians. I saw how she quietly and patiently opened to the suggestions offered, her willingness to give it a try. A leader listens, and she did and still does.

I have had the pleasure of working with her as a COM Board President these last 9 months, during the COVID 19 pandemic. We have had many hurdles and challenges to address. Glenda has stepped up to the demands putting in many zoom hours and phone conversations as we tackled some very difficult scenarios. I experienced Glenda as a team player, a woman of integrity as we worked collaboratively for the greater good of all. We as a Board, have had a front row seat witnessing the immense value in how her presence, her energy, her patience has made a positive contribution to our many, many zoom meetings.

Hannelore chose well, and I am grateful for our Director, Glenda.

Love,

Susan DeLorenzo

9 - Attend A Circle Celebration

Join Us for Sunday Celebration - 10:00 – 11:30 AM

Sunday Celebration is a celebration of hope, life, and of each other and ourselves as the divine beings we indeed are. Every Sunday, we gather at 10:00 -11:30 AM, with social time until noon. (During Covid Celebration is only on - Zoom. The link below.)We invite you to join us on all Sundays. All are welcome!

Each week a different inspirational speaker shares their message, personal spirituality, wisdom, and inspiration on various subjects, personal life experiences, and how they, and we, can deal with whatever might be going on in our world. Every week is uniquely different. There is time for questions and comments, music, and three beautiful prayers.

We hope to meet you soon at Sunday Celebration or at one of the other events or workshops which are listed in the Circle website Calendar https://circleofmiracles.org/

Zoom Link is the same every Sunday and is available on the website Calendar.
 Meeting ID: 816 6107 0026 Passcode: 626150

Zoom Link:
https://us02web.zoom.us/j/81661070026?pwd=QmtTaGVtMjRYT3c4aUt5a0EwTmVHUT09

10 - Celebration Program

Circle of Miracles

AN INTERSPIRITUAL COMMUNITY

Sunday Celebration Program
10:00 AM – 11:30 AM

Mission Statement

Music (Please write your intentions now.)

Opening Prayer:

I now ask the innermost center of my being
to release all negativity from the week just passed,
and throughout my life.
I let go of angry feelings and disturbing emotions.
I remove from my mind thoughts of doubt,
fear, guilt, and judgment.
I firmly discharge any beliefs of inadequacy,
ill health, or scarcity.
Beginning this very moment,
I allow myself to see the world as a possibility of goodness,
peace, and harmony.
I patiently look for good intentions, gentleness, and cooperation.
I find evidence of health, forgiveness, joy, and abundance.
I replace fear with love.
Because I sow strong, vigorous seeds of positive expectations,
carefully water and nourish them
by making an optimistic attitude part of my life,
the Divine Creative Force within me
grows a bountiful harvest from the very seeds I have sown.
And so it is so!

Spiritual Seed

Speaker/Spark
Sharing/Interaction with Speaker

Guided Meditation &
A Moment of Healing & Gratitude

Music

Declaration:
I am a Free Spiritual Being,
manifested from the Source of all life.
That is my true identity.
No person, place, or thing can hold power over me.
The unlimited wisdom and supply of my Source
is always flowing powerfully within me.
I choose to access this great Intelligence,
and live my life in harmony
with Its gentle, internal guidance.
Freedom is accepting my unique Self.
Freedom is letting go of my judgments,
and allowing others to affect their own destinies.
Freedom is lightheartedness,
and finding abundance everywhere.
Freedom is creating miracles with love, joy, and laughter.
Freedom is knowing that I really am Divine!
And, remembering who I am,
I extend my hand and lovingly ask you to walk with me,
in freedom, harmony, and peace.

Announcements

Closing Prayer:
Heavenly Creator, Divine Consciousness,
We welcome You into our awareness,
and open ourselves to Your loving guidance.
Awaken our direction in life
to the Universal Will of Your peaceful perfection.
We thank You for the blessings in our lives,
and for seeing only our innocence.
Through Your presence in our hearts,
guide us in the light of Your Love,

93

in co-creation with the Divine Plan.
Amen

Closing Song: Now There Is Peace On Earth (notice changes in wording)

Social Time: 11:30 AM-12:00 Noon
A chance to connect with the Circle community, and the speaker.
All are welcome!!

11 - Attend Circle Ministry School

If you have questions, comments or would like to request a catalog or application, please email info@circleofmiracles.org or call 267-218-4254 for more information.

School facilitators and former students are happy to speak with you at any time!

12 - Reverend Mike Wanner

Rev. Mike Wanner started his metaphysical and ministerial studies with Reiki in 1993 and had studied seven styles of Reiki in the U.S., Japan, Canada, Denmark, and Australia. He is certified to teach.

He became certified to teach Integrated Energy Therapy in 1999 and co-taught the new millennium's first IET class. Mike began dowsing in 2001.

Ordained as an Interfaith Minister of the Circle of Miracles Ministry and a Metaphysical Minister of the International Metaphysical Ministry, Rev. Mike practices and teaches spiritual energy therapies in the Philadelphia Area.

He was a faculty member of the Medical Mission Sister's Center for Human Integration's School of Integrated Body/Mind Therapies in Fox Chase, Philadelphia, PA, for twelve years.

For a complete Biography, please visit
http://ReverendMikeWanner.com/Bio

Free Kindle Books

☥

Free Healing Books

https://angelraphaelspeaks.com/healing-presents/

Free Cancer Books

https://angelraphaelspeaks.com/free-cancer-books/

Free Prison Books

https://angelraphaelspeaks.com/christmas/

www.ingramcontent.com/pod-product-compliance
Lightning Source LLC
Chambersburg PA
CBHW060403050426
42449CB00009B/1875